BRAINPOWER

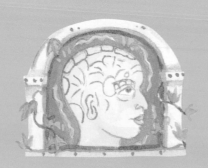

BRAINPOWER

PRACTICAL WAYS TO BOOST YOUR MEMORY, CREATIVITY AND THINKING CAPACITY

Laureli Blyth

BARNES
&NOBLE
BOOKS
NEW YORK

Contents

Introduction

BrainPower is a book about understanding and using the whole brain to improve your life. By optimizing the use of your brain, you can achieve better memory, increased creativity, and improved thinking capacity. You will also better understand your unconscious and the connection your thoughts have on your feelings and actions.

You don't have to be a neurologist to understand how to use your brain. You can discover how to effectively unlock the power of the mind while finding the most important keys to achieving your greatest desires.

Over the last century, major breakthroughs have been made that have simplified the mysteries of the brain so that now it is a simple-to-use system.

In this book, we will focus on how to learn. The emphasis is on the activation of neurological processes. We learn and remember by experience, and experience is a neurological process. Important to this process is the mind–body connection — the influence of emotional balance, the effect of a high-energy diet, and the function of physical health and mental exercise.

The brain is like a muscle. When you use it, it grows and your mind produces results. As you develop your mental capabilities, you learn things more easily. When you first use a muscle that hasn't been exercised much, it gets sore. But, if you keep doing your exercises, it adapts and gets stronger. This also applies to the brain.

An essential part of this book is devoted to the higher conscious mind. It is important to know and understand how to work with this part of the brain — sometimes called the wise and knowing mind. The conscious, thinking mind, often over-analyzes and leads us to become stuck or irrational, while the unconscious mind is only as functional as the "programs" it stores.

This book provides simple yet powerful techniques for you to follow. It will help you toward a better life by allowing you to get rid of unwanted habits and thinking patterns. You will have a clearer, more powerful and strong, "whole" brain.

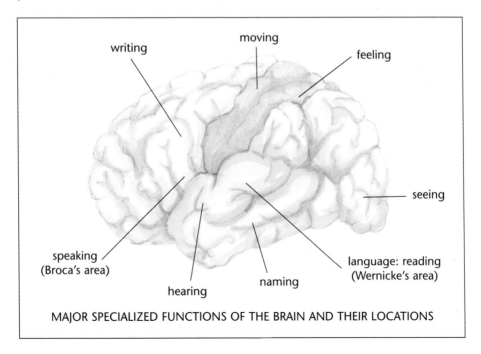

MAJOR SPECIALIZED FUNCTIONS OF THE BRAIN AND THEIR LOCATIONS

Maximize the Power
of Your Brain

Imagine understanding how your brain works so it empowers you with knowledge and tools that give you limitless capabilities to have the life you want, and ultimately, were meant to have. Your brain has virtually unlimited power to function, to do, and to be all it can imagine and more. By engaging it and operating from a point of contemplative control, you can get maximum results.

Though the brain is like a muscle, it is much more than that. Your brain has an operating system much like a computer's. The difference lies in the programming, or what is called soft-wiring capabilities. Your brain serves as a liaison organ with the body. It is the link between the thoughts generated in the mind and the body's awareness or "memory" of these thoughts. The brain maintains this awareness throughout the rest of the body. To understand how this works, see page 12, The Nervous System.

As humans, we begin our programming at our conception. Our environment, culture, values, beliefs, parents, friends, teachers and peers all shape our soft-wiring or programs. This means that as you grow, move, change and make choices, your programs or ways you live and believe, can — and do — change. It's like installing a new program in a computer. Once programs are installed, they work automatically or unconsciously. With **BrainPower** you will learn how to reprogram your brain to have the life you want. Most importantly, it will teach you how to let go of your old programs before installing your new ones, to avoid conflict in trying to run both old and new programs at the same time. Sound familiar? This is where we have often gone astray in our programming abilities.

THE QUALITY OF YOUR LIFE IS THE OUTCOME OF YOUR OWN THOUGHTS.

THE BRAIN OPERATING SYSTEM

The brain operating system runs without your thinking mind being aware of it. It is a magnificent, organized structure that surpasses any imaginable sophisticated computer in the universe. As you read through this list, you may notice it is not comprehensive of all the functions of your brain; however, it does highlight the significant components.

- Serves as a liaison between the mind's thoughts and the body's physiology and neurology.
- Generates waves of energy, or *ergs*, as it responds to thoughts.
- Functions as a sorter-reasoning-intellectualizing component, that forms our opinions from the data that is held in our existing programs or minds.
- Gathers information that comes in via the five physical senses, which are stimulated by the environment.
- Attracts and/or repels, depending upon your thought.
- Stores and surfaces back-learned material, to remember learned information when needed for "now," and interprets it in a meaningful way.
- Governs the body for the nervous system.
- Generates a "Consciousness."
- Holds most of its data in the unconscious mind.
- Controls body temperature, blood pressure, heart rate, and breathing.
- Handles physical motion when walking, talking, standing, and sitting.
- Allows you to think, dream, reason and experience emotions.

WHEN PEOPLE KNOW BETTER, THEY DO BETTER.

Where are the Programs?

First, know the different functions of the mind. This helps you to access them for improved functionality and maximized brainpower.

The basic Brain Operating System is made up of Three Minds, which work together simultaneously.

The mind or intelligence is "*thought*," and is an invisible source that flows through the human brain as a vibrational frequency.

There is a connection between the body and mind and spirit.

The Brain is a complex mechanism that is linked to the physical body through the emotions. Therefore, it can be said that thoughts reside in many areas and parts of your body and may have an effect on aches, pains, diseases and mental problems.

Life is an "out-picturing" of what is stored and programmed in the unconscious mind.

Life is like a giant screen on which our lives are projected. We cannot change the outer projection, unless we change our inner programs. We communicate with the unconscious mind by going within, and using our imagination and inner vision.

CHANGE YOUR THINKING AND CHANGE YOUR LIFE. William James

THE THREE MINDS

If you want to know what is in your unconscious mind, just look at your life and your world, as the unconscious mind is "out-picturing" (ie projecting) your beliefs, thoughts, and values about yourself and others.

All three minds give you the external, outer world — the "screen of life" — as your experience, ie how you see, hear, feel, smell, and taste.

Higher Conscious Mind
Knowingness, intuition,
open to higher awareness

Unconscious Mind
Storehouse for memories, emotions, habits and behaviors. *The unconscious mind can get information from your higher conscious mind, and pass it on to the conscious mind.*

Conscious Mind
Thinking, judging, analyzing,
doing and choosing

REMEMBER We have the free will to think our own thoughts, which gives us domain over our lives.

THE NERVOUS SYSTEM

Your nervous system exists throughout the mind and body. Through neurology — the scientific study of the nervous system — we know that the brain receives data from internal organs, and transmits messages back to those organs. Each area of nerves has its own chemical formula, amps of electricity and power capabilities. Through the nervous system, nerves set up a magnetic field controlled by the chemicals of the body. The brain is the center of this magnetic field, and it is controlled by the conscious, higher conscious and unconscious thought impulses. Thus, emotions trigger the chemicals that activate the system. In the nervous system:

- ⊙ Thoughts are the electricity of the system
- ⊙ Emotions are the magnetism of the system
- ⊙ The chemicals come from how you hold your body.

All three are necessary for the function of your nervous system.

Thoughts produce chemicals, and as you change your thoughts and language, you change your physiology and neurology. Whether you know it or not, your brain is constantly making neurological connections. For our brains to function effectively, messages are relayed from one nerve cell to the next. This is achieved by special chemicals called **neurotransmitters**. Memory, learning, comprehension, moods, emotions and all mental processes are dependent on adequate supplies of brain chemicals and neurotransmitters. The body is full of neurological connections that form pathways, most of which function on automatic pilot.

Neurons are the working elements of the thinking regions of the brain and the brain is comprised of 180 billion such cells. It is here that memories are stored. Each neuron is an electrical impulse and is like an individual information processing system. A neuron holds our thoughts in its cells. A combination of these neurons forms to provide our nervous system.

Changing Your Thought Patterns

We often live with our problems until we can't stand them any longer, either through frustration, disgust or pain. Sometimes divorce, death or separation spurs change. Imagine now, taking control. The only person who can do this for you is you. Habitual thoughts and feelings can be changed. You only need to begin to consciously retrain these thoughts.

If you have ever had an accident and had physiotherapy, or wanted to train yourself in a new behavior, you may have realized that in order to produce results, you need to have repetition in thought, movement and action. Often, parts of the nervous system become redundant due to misuse or non-use of a skill or activity. Sometimes, outside forces come into our lives that can block connections and pathways.

Things that inhibit neurotransmitters

❋ Smoking ❋ Drugs ❋ Drinking ❋ Oxygen deprivation
❋ Stress ❋ Depression ❋ Unchallenging environments
❋ Strokes ❋ Traumatic physical accidents

Building New Neurological Connections

- ⊙ Be aware that you are the one in charge and in control of your life and your thoughts.
- ⊙ Consciously change your mind and thoughts, and you will notice how it will change your physical and emotional state.
- ⊙ Take action. Decide how you wish to be, and begin being that. Practice. The key is repetition, repetition, repetition. Practice it at the same time everyday. Spend at least 10–30 minutes or more.
- ⊙ Change the way you hold your body and breath as you do the activity. Be confident in mind, breathe deeply, and believe that you can do it.
- ⊙ If an unwanted thought comes in, say to it "cancel, erase and go away!" Decide what you'd rather think instead. If you have to do this a hundred times at first, then do it. Think of it as a needle going over an old record, and as you cancel/erase, you are reapplying the needle to the track you wish to play. The negative chatter will become less, and finally stop.

Physical and mental action literally builds new neurological connections. The process can be hard and sometimes painful, but once made, the new pathway will become automatic.

REMEMBER Your mind has the ability to self-organize, self-stabilize, self-replicate, self-reference, self-mirror and self-modify.

COMMUNICATING WITH YOUR UNCONSCIOUS MIND

You may wish to read this exercise aloud and record it – play it back and listen, allowing yourself to relax and go into a trance, or have someone else read it to you. Either way, it should be read in a gentle, trance-inducing voice.

✻ Close your eyes and relax ... concentrate on your breathing. Be aware of the rhythm of your chest moving in and out, and of your body relaxing and going deeper with each breath. As you continue to breathe, imagine you are on a path in a very lush, beautiful forest. All around you are thick green trees and flowers. Let yourself be there as you walk, almost glide, down this pathway towards the sound of water. Let yourself go to this safe, pleasant place now.

✻ Imagine you are now at the place of this water, and you go over and look at your reflection. (Pause.) Imagine that you feel someone standing next to you ... feel completely safe, and you see his or her reflection in the water, too. You know this is the reflection of your unconscious mind.

✻ Allow yourself to sit down in the soft grass by the water, and be in the company of your unconscious mind. Let yourself realize you are part of this reflection. Just send it thoughts of love and gratitude for all it does for you.

✻ As you are relaxing and trusting even more, imagine the unconscious mind is available for you to get more clarity and direction. Let whatever you need to know, or wish to do something about, be spoken. Await the response.

✻ Let your unconscious mind know you wish to make change, and enlist its assistance in this endeavor now. Ask your unconscious mind to start this process now, and to allow you to have an increasing awareness of having made those changes now.

As you do this exercise, you are communicating with your unconscious mind and retraining your neurology to rethink, and to refeel, in new ways.

Intelligence Boosters

THE MAGIC OF WHOLE-BRAIN THINKING

Whole-brain thinking is a process that allows you to manage your own mind at all levels, and to develop excellence as you access your personal genius.

The magic of whole-brain thinking is held in the two functioning sides or hemispheres of our brain. These two hemispheres have four quadrants. Each of these quadrants is specialized for its own type of thinking.

A person can **iterate,** or go back and forth, between the four modes within the brain to get useful solutions to situations and problems. We do this unconsciously and constantly. We can also learn how to do this **"consciously"** to awaken our genius, creative self.

Overall creativity is a whole-brain process.

The brain hemispheres have their own functions and operate semi-independently, even though they are physically connected.

- ⊙ **The Left Brain**, for most people, is dominant. The left seems to control mental functions required for logical and scientific thinking.
- ⊙ **The Right Brain** specializes in perceptions and concepts. It is abstract and metaphoric.

Whether left-brain thoughts or right-brain thoughts, both generate electrical impulses or pure energy (ergs), which automatically send out a negative or positive current that is chemically propelled and sets up magnetic fields. This enables you to repel or attract energies into your world or field of perception.

This is the process of awakening the genius brain.

As you learn to cultivate the personal mastery over your mind and emotions consciously, you will begin to acquire whole-brain thinking.

The two hemispheres of the brain are hard-wired together by the *corpus callosum,* and the two halves of the limbic system are joined by the *hippocampal commisure.*

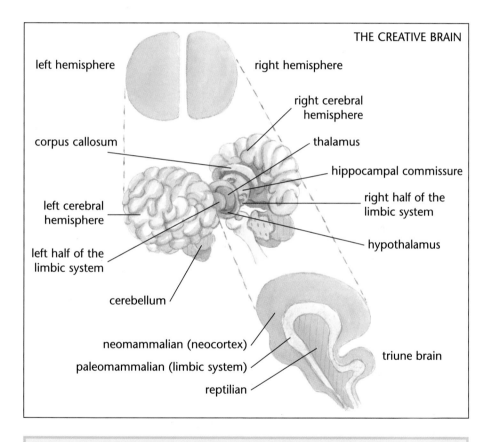

THE CREATIVE BRAIN

left hemisphere

right hemisphere

right cerebral hemisphere

corpus callosum

thalamus

hippocampal commissure

left cerebral hemisphere

right half of the limbic system

left half of the limbic system

hypothalamus

cerebellum

neomammalian (neocortex)

paleomammalian (limbic system)

triune brain

reptilian

GENIUS, IN TRUTH, MEANS LITTLE MORE THAN THE FACULTY OF PERCEIVING IN AN INHABITABLE WAY. WILLIAM JAMES

Creative expansion comes from learning to listen to and trust our intuition or hunches of the right brain, while following the logic and verification of the left brain.

- Imagine being only right-brained. We would only have pipe dreams or weird ideas and thoughts that would be difficult to apply.
- Imagine being only left-brained. We would only have rigid processes that would be draining and boring to live with.

Left Brain:
- Its main purpose is the conversion of perceptions into logic and phonetic depictions of reality.
- It deals with thinking, language, reading, counting and all digital communications. It is referred to as the verbal hemisphere.
- It controls the right side of the body.
- It assists in keeping the right brain balanced.

Right Brain:
- It controls the functions used in artistic thinking, such as music, dancing, painting and sculpting.
- It is intuitive and symbolic, holistic, integrating and creative.
- It controls the left side of the body.

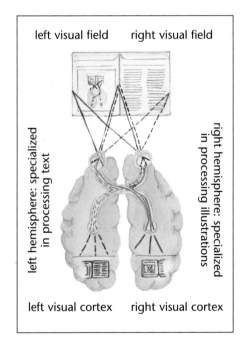

left visual field   right visual field

left hemisphere: specialized in processing text

right hemisphere: specialized in processing illustrations

left visual cortex   right visual cortex

Note: If you are dominant left-brained, you are normally right-handed. The role of the right-brain hemisphere is essential to the creative process. It supplies only a quarter of the thinking. We need the left hemisphere and both halves of the limbic system to optimize creative output.

Brain Booster Exercises
to activate and build your brainpower

Doing these simple exercises daily allows you to access one brain hemisphere while in another.

Cross-over Connect

- Stand or sit, and put your right hand across your body to your left knee as you raise that knee, and then do the same thing with your left hand on your right knee, just as if you are marching. Do this for at least 2 minutes.

Cross-over Surface

As quickly as possible:

- Touch and name 10 items in the room.
- Touch the same 10 items giving them a name that they are not; for example, touch a chair and name it a table.

Infinity Flow

- In the air, draw an imaginary infinity sign with your finger.
- Trace it in the air three to four times
- Now trace it in the reverse direction three to four times.

Neurological Hook-up

- Stand or sit with your right leg over your left leg at the ankles.
- Put your right wrist over your left wrist, link and clasp your fingers so that your right wrist is on top.
- Bend your elbows and gently turn your fingers in towards the body until they rest in the center of your chest, on your breast bone. Keeping your ankles and wrists crossed, breathe evenly while in this position for at least 60 seconds.

Consciously practicing these exercises allows you to expand your intelligence and awaken the genius brain.

AWAKEN THE GENIUS BRAIN

What is genius? It is the ability to produce new things of great complexity from a set of fixed, simple energies. Genius is the ability to go beyond those rules and think about them, question them, modify them, and produce incredible results.

From where does genius come? It comes from nature and the behaviors of pattern. The difference between those who have extraordinary human intelligence and creativity and those who don't is that, the mind of a genius can step outside a set of fixed rules and create new responses and rules. Genius is not an all or nothing phenomenon. It is not something we have or do not have. It is developed by degrees, and as a direct result of using our whole brain. It reflects how we choose to incorporate ideas and patterns as we use and replicate them.

Is being a genius learnable, or it is something with which you were born? We all know people who intuitively seem to be able to access whole-brain thinking. How we are born is not how we have to be. If we do not use our abilities, they often cease to function; similarly, when we begin using abilities, they grow and expand.

Can genius be explicitly taught? It can be taught, if we design our educational material while taking into account the critical need of combining the process and the content of what we teach; then genius is available to everyone.

The process of awakening the genius brain is to exercise it. Learn to cultivate personal mastery over your mind and emotions consciously; then you will begin to use whole-brain thinking and the genius brain.

Exercising The Genius Brain

This exercise trains your mind to consciously think in whole-brain, creative patterns. When you do this, you are using the genius brain. The more you use your whole brain, the stronger it becomes.

* Put four chairs in a circle, with each chair representing a different frame of mind that corresponds to whole-brain thinking, as noted below.
* Think of something you want to achieve or have a better perspective about. Visualize, as if it were a movie, having accomplished this achievement or gained a better perspective. Allow yourself to imagine this as freely as you can.
* Starting with the rational, thinking-mind, ask the questions of this part of your mind, writing down the answers that surface.
* Continue in a clockwise manner around the chairs, while you assume each frame of mind and ask the questions.

THE RATIONAL, THINKING-MIND CHAIR

Think about the accomplished outcome you desire as you step back and imagine the BIG picture, as if from above. Then ask:
* Where will this lead me? * What will happen if I don't achieve this?

THE VISIONARY, RISK-TAKER, CURIOUS-MIND CHAIR
* What are my extraordinary gifts, talents, and abilities which I can use?
* Is there anything else I can do to make them work?
* What can I do to make them work even better?

THE SAFETY, ORGANIZED, RELIABLE-MIND CHAIR
* Are there other factors that need to be taken care of?
* How can I organize this so it has a firm foundation?
* What needs to be there for future security?

THE FEELING, EMOTIONAL, SENSITIVE-MIND CHAIR
* If no one else was involved, what would I choose to do?
* What am I really feeling, and why?
* How can I achieve what I want and be emotionally balanced?

REVIEW YOUR ANSWERS. How are you better equipped to achieve this outcome?

IMPROVE YOUR MEMORY AND CONCENTRATION

In order to memorize and concentrate, we need to have a way to consciously work with thoughts. The best method is through pictures and visualization. Train your brain to practice making pictures of what you want to remember. In ancient times, the history of a tribe or clan was memorized by a designated person. This was most probably achieved by visualizing it as a story. This is how we remember most stories: we picture them. There are two types of information that we may wish to remember.

- ⊙ **Concrete ideas:** Things that have a solid form and are usually nouns or adjectives; for example, trees, people, houses, cars, lakes, boats, etc. Concrete ideas are more tangible and easier to remember or memorize.
- ⊙ **Abstract ideas:** Things that have no substance. They describe things and are often feelings, and nominalizations. Abstract ideas often get mixed up with other abstract ideas and are harder to remember.

You can train your mind to turn your abstract ideas into pictures, which will improve your memory and concentration. When abstract and concrete ideas come together, they give form to the ideas and allow them to attract what they represent, and then to materialize.

The mind processes information in groups or chunks of 7 + 2 or 7 − 2 pieces of information at a time. (As few as 5 pieces or as many as 9 pieces). It is helpful if you group or chunk the things you wish to remember this way. Think back to when you learned the alphabet. The best way to visualize something is to see it in your mind's eye. It will not seem as real or vivid as open-eyed reality; however, to your unconscious mind, it is just as real. It is where your memory is stored and from where it is recalled.

**PEOPLE DON'T HAVE BAD BRAINS, THEY HAVE
PROGRAMS THAT DON'T FUNCTION WELL.**

MEMORY BOOSTERS

The mind remembers best in visual pictures. Memory boosters involve turning abstract ideas into solid pictures, making them into a story and storing them in the memory. When ideas or words are abstract, we can easily make them into pictures by choosing a symbol for each thought that best relates to the idea. Often, how you think or feel about the idea will determine which picture you choose. The key is to make the picture represent how you feel or think about the idea.

As you think of about the following concepts, sketch a symbol that relates to the idea.

1. Prosperity	6. Closed
2. Increase	7. Extra
3. Learn	8. Genius
4. Energized	9. Dream
5. Afraid	10. Time

String together these pictures to make a story. Repeat the story without looking at the list. This exercise allows you to remember anything – from topics for an essay or a speech, to shopping lists to step-by-step instructions. Its application is unlimited. You will remember an abstract thing by making a picture of it.

Here are some handy hints.
- ⊙ Write down the word and the related picture.
- ⊙ Make a story of all the words in list order, and visualize it happening.
- ⊙ Recall the key words in the story by making them especially colorful, action-packed, and vivid, even outlandish.
- ⊙ Store the story or movie in the "Visual Remember" part of your mind. (Upper right if left-handed, and upper left if right-handed.)
- ⊙ Recall the key words as you think of the story, and notice how well you remember them.

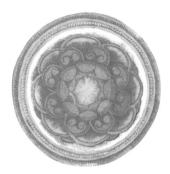

Often, when we want to travel or go somewhere, we make a mental image of the route we will take before we begin our journey. It is so often unconscious or automatic that we are not even aware we do this.

To boost your memory, you need to have a way of retrieving the information you wish to remember.

To remember means to go back into your collective memory and bring the related data and information to the forefront of your mind. Often, we have so much clutter there, it is hard to recover the desired memory.

A great exercise for boosting your memory involves remembering people's names. It gives your mind a disciplined way to file information in a logical, simple-to-retrieve manner. To learn this method expands our memory in multiple dimensions.

Ever feel a bit forgetful? You could probably use more water.
It is our hydration that keeps our neurology flowing.
There are scientific laboratories in the world that have showers off the labs specifically for rehydrating the body and ultimately the brain cells. This gives the scientists fresh ideas.

Remembering People's Names

A very effective way to remember someone's name and information about him or her, takes only a few seconds upon the first initial meeting. This can be done by relaxing and taking your time and allowing your unconscious mind to absorb the information.

- ⊙ As you meet people, look them in the face and repeat their names, either to yourself or out loud. If you cannot picture a name in your mind, or it is an unusual name, have the person spell it so you can record it visually.
- ⊙ Store the name in the upper-left part of your mind if you are right-handed, and upper right if you are left-handed.
- ⊙ If there is something interesting about the person you may wish to recall later, then make a visual picture of him or her doing a task related to what you wish to remember.
- ⊙ Practicing this exercise will improve your ability to unconsciously and automatically remember names.

VISUAL REMEMBERING

If you are left handed, after visualizing the name you wish to remember, look to the upper right to store the name.

If you are right handed, after visualizing the name you wish to remember, look to the upper left to store the name.

Opening the Memory Channels

Eye movements reflect how we internally process information. They also reflect where we store and retrieve information. By doing this eye-movement exercise, you can improve your concentration and memory.

Through our nervous system, our eyes play an important part in accessing our memories and the creative ability to think and change patterns.

Exercising the eyes improves vision, as it stretches the muscles and strengthens the eye organ. It opens new neurological pathways for learning and managing our internal representations. The results you can achieve are unlimited – everyone who does eye-movement exercises experiences improved memory. The following sequence will access the different parts of your mind, improving your memory and concentration.

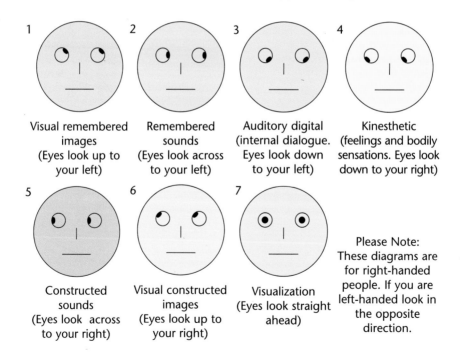

1 Visual remembered images
(Eyes look up to your left)

2 Remembered sounds
(Eyes look across to your left)

3 Auditory digital
(internal dialogue. Eyes look down to your left)

4 Kinesthetic
(feelings and bodily sensations. Eyes look down to your right)

5 Constructed sounds
(Eyes look across to your right)

6 Visual constructed images
(Eyes look up to your right)

7 Visualization
(Eyes look straight ahead)

Please Note:
These diagrams are for right-handed people. If you are left-handed look in the opposite direction.

Turbo-charged Memory Booster

Doing this exercise daily opens and builds your neurological pathways, and creates new channels for thoughts and ideas to flow through. This exercise is extremely powerful for people who have had a mild stroke or brain damage, or who are becoming forgetful. It can be painful at first, but practice makes it stronger and easier. The added benefit is a stronger eye muscle and possible eyesight improvement. Repeat the pattern a few times to get a sense of how it effects you.

Trace some of these basic shapes with your eyes:
❉ circle ❉ square ❉ X ❉ triangle
❉ now reverse all the above

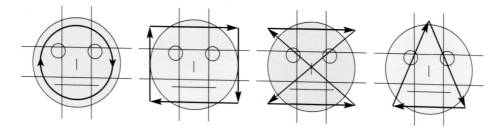

As you do these exercises, your ability to concentrate will expand
and your genius will surface.

The Magic Power of Brain Foods

Our brains are directly affected by what we put in our minds, as well as in our bodies. What we think, and how we think our thoughts, are highly valued standards to a turbo-charged brain.

A turbo-charged brain needs:

Diet, Nutrition and Exercise
- Balanced, high-brain diet
- Nutrients, vitamins and supplements
- Exercise and plenty of oxygen
- Hydration with plenty of water
- Relaxation and meditation

The adversaries of your brain are:

- Heavy-metal toxins
- Homocysteine
- Excessive animal-fat consumption
- Continual stress overload
- Free radicals

To boost your memory and protect your brain cells, you need to consume a diet rich in antioxidants. That means lots of vegetables, fruits, nuts, fish, seeds, and an adequate intake of vitamins A, C and E.

Brainpower depends on:
- regular mental and memory exercise
- antioxidant-rich diet
- daily intake of vitamins, minerals and supernutrients.

You can have a hair–mineral analysis done, which will give you a complete breakdown of the heavy-metal load and vitamin deficiencies in your body.

THE ENERGIZERS

BRAIN BOOSTER VITAMINS	Vitamin B1	Leads to forgetfulness, confusion and depression when deficient.
	Vitamin B3	Improves energy production, and is needed for a number of biochemical reactions that occur in the body.
	Vitamin B5	Considered the anti-stress vitamin.
	Vitamin B6	Activates the "memory and thinking" facility.
	Vitamin B12	Prevents nerve damage by maintaining the fatty sheath that surrounds the nerves. If deficient, leads to severe brain and nerve impairment.
	Vitamin E	Thought to ward off the memory problems associated with aging.
	Vitamin C	Thought to protect against cognitive impairment.

Vitamin Bs, which include B1,B3,B5,B6 and B12, improve cognitive memory and activity by increasing key neurotransmitters, such as acetylochline, dopamine and serotonin. Consume plenty of green vegetables, brown rice, tofu, nuts, sunflower seeds and eggs.

MINERALS	Zinc	Memory Booster	Apples, pears, beans, oysters, ginger, peas.
	Magnesium	Good for circulation and prevents calcification from eroding brain cells.	Almonds, cashews, soybeans, seafood, blackstrap molasses.
NUTRIENTS	Lecithin	From soybean oil, a good source of choline, which is the building block for acetylocholine, the neurotransmitter primarily responsible for comprehension, learning and memory.	
	Coenzyme Q10 (CoQ10)	A vitamin-like nutrient that plays a major role in energy production. Supports the body, helping to lower blood pressure and cholesterol.	
	Ginseng	Well known for its rejuvenative powers and used as an energy tonic and stimulant.	

SUPER-CHARGED MEMORY SUPERNUTRIENTS

These boost memory and promote clear memory function. Use only with the consent of your physician or medical practitioner.

Ginkgo Biloba is a herb, and a brain nutrient. It has the ability to enhance mental functions and behavior, and is often prescribed to treat memory loss.

⊙ Improves the brain's ability to use glucose for energy.
⊙ Protects the red blood cells from free radical damage with its antioxidant capabilities.
⊙ Allows safe passage of oxygen to the brain cells.
⊙ Is an anti-stress nutrient and anxiety reliever.
⊙ Is a great supplement for blood flow to the brain.

Phosphatidylserine, or **PS**, is a derivative of soy lecithin and often thought to be the best of the brain supernutrients.

⊙ Reduces the effects of stress by suppressing the hormone cortisol.
⊙ Protects cell membranes, preventing premature brain aging.
⊙ Is responsible for nerve-growth regulation, and reverses the decline of nerve growth in the memory center or hippocampus.
⊙ Has antioxidant properties and protects cells against free radicals.
⊙ Improves acetylocholine and dopamine, which boosts memory and makes you feel happy.
⊙ Improves short-term memory and the ability to maintain concentration, as well as long-term recall.

Acetyl-L-Carnitine, or **ALC**, is a nutrient that prevents premature brain aging.

⊙ Increases production of acetylcholine and dopamine, which boost learning, memory and emotional stability.
⊙ Prevents the accumulation of lipofuscin in the hippocampus by its antioxidant activity. (Lipofuscin buildup promotes the erosion of mental faculties.)

Alpha Lipoic Acid is a powerful antioxidant that protects cell membranes.
⊙ Shields the mitochondria (present in living cells, responsible for respiration and energy production) from the effects of free radicals.
⊙ Binds to heavy metals making them harmless.

Combine diet, nutrition, supplements and vitamins with relaxation techniques such as meditation. Get more oxygen by learning how to breathe deeply, and by exercising your body as you exercise your mind. Poor nutrition and lack of exercise diminish the supply of natural chemicals, and deplete the body of its nutrients.

As the physical body comes under stress and the natural aging process progresses, you can find supplements that will provide you with replacement nutrients.

HORMONES FOR ANTI-AGING

Estrogen	Improves learning and memory. Stimulates production of a nerve growth factor, which protects brain cells necessary for memory.
Dehydroepiand-rosterone (DHEA)	Is responsible for boosting energy and building bone density. Also stimulates nerve growth and the connections between nerves. Anti-aging hormone that counteracts the effects of the stress hormone cortisol. It allows the hippocampus (responsible for the memory) to function efficiently.
Human Growth Hormone (HGH)	Enhances memory.
Melatonin	Fortifies the aspects of the immune system. A hormone secreted by the pineal gland, it assists with good sleep.
Cortisol	Maintains blood pressure, and provides amino acids and glucose for energy during times of stress; is related to stress.

NOTE Use in moderation and consult a physician for best results, as some people are allergic to some supplements.

HIGH-ENERGY BRAIN DIET

	DO	DON'T
BREAKFAST	Start the day with high-protein food at least 20 minutes before you eat the rest of your breakfast. ⊙ Eggs ⊙ High-fiber cereal ⊙ Yogurt ⊙ Low-fat or skim milk ⊙ High-fiber fruits such as banana	Eat high-fat foods: ⊙ Sausages or bacon ⊙ Potatoes ⊙ White bread ⊙ Pastries ⊙ Sugars ⊙ Lots of caffeine ⊙ Skip breakfast
LUNCH	Have a high-protein lunch: ⊙ Green leafy vegetables ⊙ Legumes ⊙ Lean fish ⊙ Turkey or chicken ⊙ Grain beans, such as soybeans ⊙ Brown rice	Eat: ⊙ Bread or starchy foods ⊙ Sugar foods ⊙ Soft drinks Although such foods have a fat release that gives a temporary fix, you soon will crash and feel mentally dull.
MORNING SNACK	Eat: ⊙ Several small servings of fruits ⊙ Whole grain breads and crackers ⊙ Dried fruits	Eat: ⊙ Pure carbohydrates ⊙ Pastries, chips ⊙ Breads This leads to low blood sugar and drowsiness.

	DO	DON'T
DINNER	Ideally have one serving of lean, red meat at least three times a week to boost brain power with protein and iron. If you are a vegetarian, make sure you eat legumes such as red lentils and soy foods. ⊙ Pasta with tuna or chicken ⊙ Chicken stir fry with rice ⊙ Fresh green vegetables ⊙ Fruit ⊙ Water	Eat: ⊙ Pizzas, convenience and fast foods more than once a week. ⊙ Refined, processed, packaged foods
AFTERNOON/EVENING SNACKS	Replace junk foods and snacks with foods that break the hunger attacks. ⊙ English muffins ⊙ Fruit-bread toast ⊙ Raisins ⊙ Apples ⊙ Low-fat yogurt ⊙ Low-fat ice cream ⊙ Pita bread ⊙ Popcorn	Eat: ⊙ Potato chips ⊙ Processed snack foods and dips ⊙ Heavy whipped creams and full-fat ice creams ⊙ Chocolates ⊙ Cakes and pies
HYDRATION	Drink: ⊙ 8 glasses of water a day ⊙ Apple juice	Drink: ⊙ Coffee, which can dehydrate ⊙ Alcohol

Harmonizing the Emotional Brain

Do you consider yourself emotionally balanced? Wouldn't it be useful to have a way to remain emotionally balanced as you navigate through life's pathways?

Emotions are highly concentrated forms of energy consciousness that stimulate responses in the body.

Emotions cannot be seen or touched, but can be felt in a powerful form. They are experienced both physically and mentally. Emotions are a fundamental manifestation of the life force.

Emotional balance depends upon what **state** you are in. A state can change from moment to moment, because this too is an emotional condition. A state is a mood, the sum total of all neurological and physiological processes within you at any given moment in time. Often, we are not aware that we are displaying an emotional state. Emotional balance is about keeping all aspects of your personal experiences in the right perspective and order. To be emotionally balanced is a deliberate choice, and one about which you should feel satisfied and content.

Some people say this is the "key to life."

> **WHAT YOU CREATE TODAY, YOU REALIZE TOMORROW.**

**ONE OF THE MASTERPIECES IS TO LIVE YOUR LIFE ON PURPOSE.
LET GO OF FEAR TO SEEK AND TRULY BEGIN TO BE.**

Some people repress their emotions, keeping them at bay, or pushing them down, or covering them up. This can cause either numbness or unwanted and exhausting eruptions, neither of which constitutes emotional balance.

When we have an unpleasant experience that causes us to behave badly or in a way we would rather not behave, we can decide to change it. It is usually not enough to wish you did not respond a certain way or behave a certain way. Determining how we behave makes it is easier to change our behavior more effectively, simply by changing the emotions and states that generated those behaviors.

There are two main components to a state or emotion:

- Internal state, or how you see it, hear it and feel it internally.
- Physiological state, or how you hold and move your body externally.

THE POWER OF EMOTIONAL BALANCE

A resourceful state leads us to achieving emotional balance, a feeling of wholeness, and peace of mind. Everyone has feelings, worries, and stress, and sometimes the emotional part of us gets upset, envious or jealous and thinks the only way to live is to accept this negativity as a part of who we are or to blame someone else for it. With brainpower, you have a choice of how you want to think and be - this is the most powerful thing about the human psyche. Having control over emotions allows you to be in the flow of life. It empowers you with energy that was once bogged down with the carrying of emotional baggage.

How to Achieve Emotional Balance

- ⊙ Develop the ability to pay attention to and identify your current state or emotions. Do this by consciously being aware of how you are.
- ⊙ Choose and decide how you would rather be. Ask yourself, "How would I rather be feeling now?" Take your time; this is something we often forget to do. It has become unfamiliar.
- ⊙ Shift your body into a posture and breath in a way that complements the new state.
- ⊙ Begin thinking resourceful and corresponding thoughts about how you wish to be.

It is important to begin practicing, experiencing, controlling and assessing the emotions that you want to have. **This requires practice and diligence and will change your state and emotions.**

> WHEN WE CREATE PEACE AND HARMONY AND BALANCE IN
> OUR MINDS, WE FIND IT IN OUR LIVES. Louise Hay

RESOURCEFUL STATES

Listed are three resourceful emotional states. Begin to learn how they feel, and to adjust your physiology, emotions and behaviors to access them.

Composed:
- Picture or visualize a tranquil lake scene as you allow yourself to be there and to relax.
- Close your eyes and take a deep breath as you relax and readjust your body posture.
- Listen to slow, relaxing music inside your head.
- Lift your inner eyes to your third-eye area, and let yourself feel the peaceful tranquility.

Amused or Pleased:
- Picture or visualize a funny thing that happened that made you fall down laughing.
- Go within and smile; as you do, imagine having a sparkling smile from inside out.
- Listen to happy, energetic music and let yourself dance.
- Remember or imagine a time when you felt good about yourself, or someone else felt good about you, so it makes you smile.

Curious:
- Imagine being a small child again and being very inquisitive about how things work.
- Be very curious and wonder about how airplanes fly, or how the world is held in orbit, or how you digest food.
- Change your body posture to being more forward, listening, interested and open.

Many people do not realize or believe that they can change how they feel. They hide behind their emotions as an excuse for behaving badly. They say things like: "You know how I am, so don't make me angry." Or "I'm just an emotional person."

We often tolerate our undesired emotions or avoid situations that trigger them.

We all have and need emotions. Emotions are normal and important for our balance and harmony. It is when they are repressed and not dealt with, or kept deep inside, that they become dangerous to our well-being in body, mind and spirit.

Practicing the **Resourceful States** exercises allows you to program your neurology with the experience of being resourceful. If you should enter into a situation that usually triggers an undesirable emotional state, you can decide to go into a resourceful state by just recalling and becoming it instead. You will be more in sync with the moment and can better focus on what you want instead of having to deal with the unpleasant, unwanted emotions.

The list on the next page shows how unresolved negative emotions can be formed. Knowing this assists us in choosing to respond differently. When we have unresolved negative emotions, not only do we suffer mentally, emotionally and physically, but others are affected as well. It can become contagious. You will find that as you change how you respond, other people around you also change.

MASTERING YOUR EMOTIONS

EMOTION	INTENTION
Anger	Losing control over others and/or self, using anger as an attempt to regain it.
Anxiety	Blocking the self by paralysis to avoid getting ready for a situation.
Boredom	Not taking responsibility for your own happiness or time management.
Confusion	Blocking the mind to keep it from dealing with a situation or making a decision.
Depression	Indulging in helplessness as an escape.
Fear	Entertaining a vision of danger that has not happened.
Grief	Losing control over a source of love or attention.
Guilt	Indulging in a past situation in order to avoid taking action now.
Hate	Indulging in a misplaced expression of love.
Homesickness	Feeling the loss of source of attention and self-identity.
Hurt	Denying self of responsibility for own feelings and feeling that someone is not doing what you want them to do.
Jealousy	Feeling of inadequacy compared to a known or unknown rival.
Loneliness	Placing responsibility for your happiness on someone else.
Regret	Feeling torment because something didn't go the way you wanted.
Rejection	Experiencing an unsuccessful attempt to get approval.
Self pity	Indulging in helplessness as a substitute for self love.
Shyness	Lingering till someone tells you that you're OK.
Worry	Incapacitating the self to avoid preparing for a situation.

RELEASING EMOTIONAL BAGGAGE

Imagine participating more fully in life, and trusting yourself, the future, and your unconscious mind. These can become strong investments in your future.

We often cover our desires and passions with fear and unresolved emotions. Once we break through and begin to recognize and take charge of our lives, we begin to move forward.

Thoughts of sadness, anger, and doom may surface from time to time, and often are old patterns that you carry around like a sack of bricks. The advice is to get rid of them. If they are not working for you, they only bog you down with negativity, and can take over. Release these thoughts by deciding what you would rather think instead. Doing this creates a new pattern of behavior to say "No," cancelling and eraseing the unwanted thought, saying "I'd rather think this instead." As you create the thought you'd rather think, stay focused on what you actually want.

Learn how to take control and master your emotions. Stop letting your emotions master you.

Releasing Emotional Baggage Exercise

- ⊙ Make a list of the repressed negative emotions that you are carrying around with you or that keep recurring. Work on them one at a time.
- ⊙ Refer to the list on page 39, and ask yourself honestly, "Am I allowing this negative emotion in my life due to this reason?"
- ⊙ Go inside yourself and imagine where you hold this emotion. Point to it and imagine how it looks. What shape is it? What size is it? What texture – is it hard, soft, like a knot or a sponge?
- ⊙ Imagine pushing it out of yourself or letting it float in front of you for a moment. Let it out, and experience how good it feels to be released.
- ⊙ Ask yourself, "What would I rather have here than this emotion?" Imagine something resourceful, positive, helpful. Imagine it as something that you can put in the place of the old emotion. Put it aside for now to be placed back in a moment.
- ⊙ With the old unwanted emotion, ask it, "What were you trying to do for me? What was your positive intention?" Ask it, "Can you take that positive intention and blend it into the wholeness of my being, and release and dissolve the negative as it has no place in my world?" Watch as it dissolves and blends into the symbol of the positive resource from the previous point.

If the emotion does not want to blend, you may need to talk to it and understand it rather than feel it as the enemy. All understanding comes from the love and care you have for yourself. Be loving and patient.

TRANSFORM TO A SUCCESS STATE OF MIND

Success can mean many things to different people. The principal thing to notice is how you represent success. Consider, "What does success mean to me?"

Use your brainpower to get yourself in sync, and develop a **Success List** for the three main areas of your life:

- ⊙ Physical, health, lifestyle
- ⊙ Financial, money, career
- ⊙ Personal relationships, home, family

Now ask the following questions:

- ⊙ What are two things I could do that, if I did them regularly, would make a BIG difference to my:
  - ✽ Physical life
  - ✽ Financial life
  - ✽ Personal–relationship life
- ⊙ What will it take for me to persevere and focus on my life to be a success now?
- ⊙ Am I willing to make and keep a truthful commitment to myself to be self-aware of where I am now and where I am going?

Once you have completed these questions, take some time and find a quiet place where you will not be disturbed and do the **Success State Exercise** opposite.

Success State Exercise

- ⊙ Specify how you want to feel success. How would you hold your body in this state?
- ⊙ Allow yourself to imagine what it would be like if you fully experienced this state of success, and become it now.
- ⊙ Amplify this state, charge it with more intensity. Make it bigger, brighter, bolder, add more color, or feeling, whatever it takes to make it more powerful.

Charge it even more, and when it feels like it is all around you, allow it to also be within you, then anchor that state by lightly pressing or touching your elbow or knee, somewhere you can reapply the same touch later to reactivate this state.

- ⊙ Now, think of a time in the near future when you would like to feel this success state-of-mind, and notice how you can use it.
- ⊙ When you wish to feel this Success State, touch the spot where you anchored the state. Let the Success State flood you.

> THROW BACK THE SHOULDERS, LET THE HEART SING, LET THE EYES FLASH, LET THE MIND BE LIFTED UP, LOOK UPWARD AND SAY TO YOURSELF: NOTHING IS IMPOSSIBLE! NORMAN VINCENT PEALE

Power Tools for the Brain

In this chapter, we discover processes that utilize effortless methods to boost your brainpower.

The power of the mind is the single most important factor that separates the average from the great achievers. Although undoubtedly some aspects of mental functioning drop off with age, the brain is a remarkable organ that can develop new nerve connections and strengthen existing communication pathways at virtually any age. You can choose to stay active to reach for more, or you can just let life pass you by. Too many people think themselves into old age. What do you choose to do?

Imagine using your unique brainpower to experience things in a different way, to make new inroads, to see, to listen and to respond with insight and vigor. It does not need to take a lifetime to achieve these qualities. It takes determination, action and, above all, a receptivity from within to honor yourself and others in doing what you desire. Carl Jung, the great psychologist, once wrote, "I have often seen individuals simply outgrow a problem which had destroyed others." Perhaps they started to use their brainpower for a change.

EXERCISE THE BRAIN MUSCLE

The key to boosting brainpower is to actively take on intellectual pursuits that challenge the mind. Keep it stretched and reaching to keep it energetic and aware.

- Learn how to speed-read. Scan material by reading the first and last sentences in a paragraph to get the meaning of what is being said.
- Learn a different language. This allows both sides of your brain to establish new neurological connections, the key to building stronger mind power.
- Learn new words. Do crossword puzzles, or other word puzzles. Use new words in conversations, in writing and thinking.
- Play mental games and do calculations without a calculator. We have become brain lazy with our machines and technology. Use it or lose it.
- Learn how to play a musical instrument and even read a music score.
- Meditate and learn to clear your mind for at least 20 minutes every day. Many people are taking a 20-minute power-nap daily. They are realizing the benefits from this time out for expanded awareness and clarity of mind. The best "Ah-Ha's" come from this seemingly non-active time. Thomas Edison, Albert Einstein and Benjamin Franklin, to name a few, were devoted power-nappers.

"FOR AS A MAN THINKEST IN HIS HEART, SO IS HE." PROVERBS 23.7

THE MAGIC INFLUENCE OF MUSIC ON THE BRAIN

Music can aid and strengthen your memory while you are studying, particularly if you are learning left-brain dominant studies such as vocabulary, spelling, grammar, foreign languages or mathematics. Research shows that even-tempered background music, such as Mozart or Bach, helps to retain concentration and learning for longer periods.

Music seems to have the effect of activation on the brain with particular neurological patterns that involve right-brain activities. It opens up the right hemisphere of your brain, which is creative, intuitive, and symbolic.

Listening to the compositions of Mozart and Bach helps to "organize" brain functioning, especially the creative right-brain process associated with spatial-temporal reasoning. At the University of California's Center for Neurobiology of Learning and Memory, investigators found that 36 undergraduates from the psychology department scored eight to nine points higher on the spatial IQ test after listening to 10 minutes of Mozart's "Sonata for Two Pianos in D Major."

Research shows that if you are studying for exams, you can alleviate your stress levels by listening to Gregorian chants. The rhythms will help you to breathe deeper and avoid shallow, tense breathing, and even hyperventilation if you are too anxious.

Music has been used as a therapy at least since the time of Pythagoras. It is said he would begin each day by playing music to his students to shake off sleepiness, and before they retired to relax them. We are now rediscovering the power of music for well-being, health and mental alertness.

Music Can Raise Your Child's IQ

The very act of learning how to transform a written score into its corresponding auditory and motoric patterns of music causes the brain's neural circuitry to weave together highly complex ways of information processing. These pathways will be used over and over again for the study of other formal systems such as mathematics, language, and science. These pathways are also associated with spatial-temporal reasoning.

This is why there is such an outstanding correlation between children who study music seriously and straight-A report cards.

Music training also has the following benefits:

⊙ Improved reading and language skills, including mathematics
⊙ Clearer thinking, both linear and abstract
⊙ Improved self-esteem
⊙ Improved attitude in school
⊙ Ability to be creative
⊙ Possible higher IQ

When is the best time to study and learn?

Do all short-term learning in the morning and
long-term memory learning in the evening.

EXPAND YOUR MENTAL, EMOTIONAL AND SPIRITUAL AWARENESS WITH PERIPHERAL VISION

This simple technique has been used for centuries to relax the conscious mind and expand awareness. When you practice **Peripheral Vision**, you go beyond the illusion of time and space. It takes you to a profound state of transcendence while still connected with a conscious-thinking reality. This rapid way of reaching this higher state has a multitude of rewards.

Useful times to practice Peripheral Vision are:

- When you are at a lecture or in a learning environment, as this can open your unconscious mind to absorb information.
- If you want to take your mind off of negative thoughts, as it is almost impossible to think negative or limited thoughts in this state.
- Prior to going into a relaxing meditation.

There is some evidence that this technique may synchronize both hemispheres of the brain. It allows your unconscious and higher conscious mind to be open to new learning and listening. It helps you to remember on a deeper level. It puts you into a trance-like state.

Peripheral Vision Exercise

Open Awareness State

- ☉ Focus your eyes upward and centered, as if to look at the space between the eyebrows or third-eye area. A spot on the wall, ceiling or horizon will do.
- ☉ You will notice that there are some signs of relaxation: slower, deeper breathing and muscle tension relaxing. Keep your eyes like this for a maximum of two minutes.
- ☉ Staying relaxed with your mind relaxed, move your eyes downward. Notice that you can see in front of you, yet if you were to wave your fingers out to each of your sides, you could see that, too. This is Peripheral Vision. Continue it for as long as you like.

NOTE Do not drive a car or operate machinery in this state.

LAUGHTER IS THE BEST MEDICINE

Laughter increases feelings of control and encourages an optimistic outlook. Laughter symbolizes positive emotions – faith, hope and playfulness, as well as determination and purpose. It is a powerful biochemical drug. Studies show that laughter stimulates the immune system and offsets stress. It releases endorphins – the body's natural analgesic.

Negative emotions such as anger, sadness, fear, hurt and guilt make people feel hopeless, helpless and worthless. They have a negative effect on our body, mind and spirit by affecting our body's chemistry. Taking life less seriously and, at the same time, taking conscious control of how you decide to think will allow you to have peace of mind and a life worth living, which is priceless.

Here is a piece of psychological research that you can easily reproduce when you feel down, sad or depressed:

Simply smile at yourself in a mirror for a full five minutes. It is probably the last thing that you feel like doing, and you may find it feels strange. But, if you persevere, you will find that the smile becomes genuine – perhaps because of the thought of what a dumb thing it is to do, and how silly you must look grinning at yourself when there is nothing to grin about.

Why does this work? Because mind and body are part of the same system. What affects one affects the other. By making a small change in your body and smiling, you are able to make the corresponding change in your emotions. The saying "Fake it till you make it" never sounded so true.

WARNING
LAUGHTER IS HIGHLY INFECTIOUS AND SPREADS RAPIDLY.

SO JUST HOW DO WE LEARN?

Everything we learn goes through this process.

Unconsciously	Unskilled	We start by not even knowing we don't know
Consciously	Unskilled	We realize we don't know the task
Consciously	Skilled	We consciously start to do the task
Unconsciously	Skilled	We know how to do the task and it becomes automatic or unconscious

You don't have to think about walking, or eating, or reading, it has become automatic. By knowing and understanding the process your mind goes through to learn a task, no matter how big or small, you can use this formula to learn anything you desire. **Remember:** at first, you must consciously practice a task, then it will become unconsciously skilled. Repetition makes it automatic and establishes a pattern.

Once a task is automatic, it frees up your mind to think new things and learn other skills and tasks. Have you learned how to drive a car, or type by touch, or swim, or make a bed? Notice that you can now perform these tasks and still keep your mind open for other thoughts and tasks.

Whole-brain thinking results in creative thinking.

Programming Your Incredible Inner Mind

When people are aware of the power of their spoken words, they become very careful with their thoughts and their conversations. Words and language come in two forms. The vibratory power of words either attract or detract, and are regarded as either reactive or proactive.

- ⊙ **Reactive Language** creates an image of being a victim of external circumstances.
  Have you ever said: "I never gave it a thought." Or "I don't know."
  These are examples of reactive language. It is an unconscious admission that either an opportunity has been missed because thought was not used or a wrong action was taken because of incorrect use.

- ⊙ **Proactive Language** creates positive choices about handling situations.
  What would happen if instead you said: "I will start thinking about it now." Or: "I do know, I'm working on it now." These are examples of proactive language.

Learn how to speak and direct your life with the words that will enhance your life. When you do this, you relate to yourself and communicate with others like a Master.

It has been recognized that positive reinforcement and proactive words can change the structure of our brain. When there is positive reinforcement, seratonin (a chemical that induces a sense of well-being) is released into the brain and intestines.

How simple it is to STOP and listen to what you say and take a look at your life. Are these reactive language statements keeping you stuck or somewhere you'd rather not be? It is not being a Pollyanna that works; rather, it's being responsible for what we say, and how we act and live.

Your unconscious mind listens to everything you say and think. It is a servant who follows the orders of what is programmed by these thoughts and statements. If you said "He makes me sick," or "I feel like I'm carrying the world on my shoulders," how do you think your unconscious mind would accommodate that? Most probably, with you feeling sick, with tense shoulders and a heavy back.

Knowing how powerful the mind and body connection is, and how effectively we can each begin to be the Writer, Director and Star of our lives, would you not want to begin using the tools you have, now?

We can begin to construct powerful affirmations that program our minds and redirect our lives. To affirm anything is to assert positively that it is so, even in the face of all contrary evidence. Another wonderful bonus is that affirmations put us in conscious contact with the higher conscious mind, which quickens and releases the intuitive light and energy stored in the higher conscious mind.

Perception is Projection.

THE SECRET STRENGTH OF POSITIVE WORDS

The purpose of saying affirmations and powerful words is to train the mind. The secret of making an affirmation is to say with confidence, feeling and belief the statement or assertion. By affirming, you can align yourself to be in the flow of life. The word is filled with magic and power. Words are the clothing of thoughts and manifest our expressions.

Designing your own affirmations will give you the most powerful results.

- ⊙ Decide what you wish to change, and make an affirmative statement about it.
- ⊙ State and write the affirmation in the positive, as if it is now. Don't fall into the trap of saying it will happen, or is going to happen; declare it as if it were already happening.
- ⊙ Have the affirmation written down somewhere so you can see it and reaffirm it many times daily. Some people keep their affirmations in the bathroom on sticky notes, or on the car dash board or office wall.

REMEMBER Affirmations work whether they are positive or negative. We often affirm negative statements; now you can consciously stop doing that and start using positive ones to alter your life.

THOU SHALT ALSO DECREE A THING, AND IT SHALL
BE ESTABLISHED UNTO THEE. Job 22:28

PRACTICAL AFFIRMATIONS

- ⊙ I am harmonious, energized and poised. I now draw to myself my power and good.
- ⊙ The road is clear for my peace and prosperity to come to me now.
- ⊙ I release the past and live in the infinite, wonderful now.
- ⊙ There are no lost opportunities, because, as one door shuts, another opens wide.
- ⊙ The genius within me is now released. I now fulfill my destiny.
- ⊙ Every day in every way, I get better and better.
- ⊙ Every cell in my body is healthy, happy and well.
- ⊙ Abundance through me blesses and multiplies all that I give and all that I receive.
- ⊙ Today is the first day of the rest of my life.

Sometimes, one-liners or even one phrase spoken at the right moment, can change your outlook and your mind.

THE INFLUENCE OF UNIVERSAL LAWS
ON THE MIND–BODY CONNECTION

Every society and culture has a tradition of explaining the connection between the world and humans. A simple way to define the underlying principles of this connection is the paradigm of four "**Universal Laws.**" They are the glue that holds the world and humans together.

These Laws have energies that are invisible but powerful. They put you in alignment with being a part of the oneness of the Universal Forces. When we understand and learn to work with these Laws with clarity, we reap the benefits of harmony with ourselves while being part of flow of the Universe.

Opposite are four Universal Laws that represent a significant correlation with the way in which you program and direct your life.

The Universal Laws

THE LAW	THE FUNCTION
The Law of Attraction	This law relates to the idea that positive thoughts equate to positive outcomes; and negative thoughts to negative outcomes. Just as atoms of compatibility gather together to form matter – the "like attracts like" scientific phenomena – so too do thoughts project a like reality. "As a man thinks, so he is."
The Law of Cause and Effect	For every action there is a reaction, equal in force but opposite in nature. Some people refer to this as karma. When you realize this and take responsibility for your every action, your life improves.
The Law of Free Will	Every person has the freedom of choice of how they wish to be or how they react to circumstances or events. Because of this, people are totally in charge of their bodies and daily experiences. Free will is humankind's main tool for learning lessons for evolvement.
The Law of Intention	Intention is the strongest element of every action of conduct. The behavior behind every intention is what drives it. This is why when people say they want to do something but quit or fall short, we know that their intention was not strong enough.

PROGRAM MANAGER

If you were to decide today what you want in your future, what would it be?

The secret lies in knowing what you want. We all know what we don't want, and it's in the programming of our minds to start focusing on what we do want. That is when we start to get results. It does not have to be exact, just a general direction, and the ideas will start the process.

Have you noticed that your past comes along with you into your future, until you resolve it and let it go? It's like being on an escalator in constant motion, moving from the past, going moment by moment in to the future. To leave the past behind, to put what you have learned into practice, and to go forward with excitement, anticipation and gusto is the way to approach your future.

Life is energy. Life is Spirit. Our job is to focus our energy on the patterns and things we choose, and not diffuse it by allowing it to scatter in all directions. As we set and achieve goals, life takes on meaning, and we discover that success follows success. One goal leads to another, and we find that we are happiest and most content when cooperating and in the flow of life through this creative process.

To be in the "flow" or "zone" is the ultimate experience for many people. They are so absorbed in what they are doing and being that they forget about what they are doing and being. They become "in the moment." Until you find that niche, you often feel in the grind. Which would you rather choose?

Decide what you want

- ⊙ What is the state of mind you require to get what you want?
- ⊙ Can it be achieved by being in a positive, expectant state?
- ⊙ Are you able to keep yourself on target, be flexible and make adjustments as you go?

The art of using the power of our brain and mind to live in wholeness comes through the ability to notice when we are stuck in an unproductive mindset, to become aware of the mental movies that limit our creativity, and to make new choices.

The two keys to inner harmony are **awareness** and **choice**. With this in mind do the following:

- ⊙ List all the things you Do want.
- ⊙ List all the thing you have Now to begin.
- ⊙ List all the things you Require to begin.
- ⊙ List all the things you Do Not want, and are now ready to get rid of.

Apollo 11, which took Neil Armstrong to the moon in 1969, was on-course for only three percent of the time. It managed to land on the moon and hit its desired target because its position was constantly monitored and corrected.

Program management is about constantly reviewing our actions, behaviors, moods and their consequences, and making corrections and changes to reach our goals.

QUANTUM RESULTS WITH MIND MAINTENANCE

Your life can be full of joy and happiness. You can have peace of mind, improved health, abundance and prosperity. These statements may seem exaggerated, but are based on results that people do achieve.

It is a shame that some people allow themselves to be beaten by the challenges and difficulties of life, but it is also quite needless.

As you use these brainpower tools, you can change your life. There is a ripple effect that flows outward, touching and affecting people in your life and in the universe.

We start our days very unconsciously with a shower or bath, we brush our teeth and groom ourselves, then we step out of our homes and allow the day take us where it may. Imagine what would happen if you were to start your day by envisioning your best result:

- ⊙ Have an intention for the day
- ⊙ Eat according to a high-energy brain diet
- ⊙ Use proactive language
- ⊙ Say your affirmations
- ⊙ Act as if you are who you want to be
- ⊙ Be kind to yourself and others
- ⊙ Remember you are in charge of your mind, therefore your results.

This allows you to finish your day with even better results than you envisioned.

PROGRAMMING THE FUTURE

- ⊙ State your goal so that it is positive, realistic and desirable, as well as something to which you can be committed.
- ⊙ Decide what the evidence of achieving your goal will be. What is the last thing that will happen just before you get it, or the first thing that happens right after you achieve it?
- ⊙ Make a visual picture of this outcome in your mind. Make the picture colorful, bright and big. Make sure you are in the picture, feeling how good it feels, seeing what you see, and hearing what you hear as you achieve your goal. Make it very compelling. (It may be helpful to close your eyes to make visual pictures.)
- ⊙ Then step or float out of the visualized picture so that you are looking at it like a photograph or movie.
- ⊙ Imagine taking this picture and placing it in your future. Ask your unconscious mind to assist you, then take it to where it is to manifest, and let it go. Let it go and watch as it floats down to the exact right place.
- ⊙ Open your eyes and come back to the now.

Energize your desired future by beginning to act as if you have it now. Reality follows imagination and mental imagining.

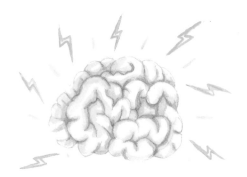

Get Inspired –
Open Your Imagination
and Intuition

The body, mind and emotions work together to create our connectedness. Through this connection, we can discover a sense of freedom to create, imagine and communicate with our higher conscious mind.

Our higher conscious mind is the part of our mind that links us with the expansive higher dimension of thought. When we allow our thoughts to go outside the square, it gives us a more vital, creative, and inspiring life.

This is the most important part of our mind to develop. We use it unwittingly, often getting those flashes of inspiration and knowingness. But imagine how empowering it is to build a personal relationship with that part of your mind.

We activate it when we are in a trance-like state of mind, when the body is relaxed, and the mind is free from internal chatter. This is often called the Inner Silence, Inner Voice or Inner State.

Sometimes, when you are facing an important decision in life, thinking about it a lot and struggling with the decision, you may notice that answers come when you slow down and seek help from within.

When you turn within, you open your imagination and intuition, which enables you to:

- Learn how to consciously take challenges into your inner silence, and get inspiration and a sense of the direction or right way to proceed.
- Learn to distinguish your inner voice from the voice of fear or ego, which often keeps us stuck.
- Learn to listen to your inner heart and intuition, to hunches, and not to what other people's fears or limitations are.
- Learn to follow your own path and intuition.

How will I recognize my inner voice?

Ultimately, you will learn how to hear your inner knowing voice or how to sense it. It usually speaks from the same area in your head or around your head, or from a place in your heart or gut. The voice tone is usually quiet and firm. Here are a few handy guidelines to further assist you in knowing if the guidance from your inner voice is right.

- If it results in a winning situation for everyone involved, chances are it's right.
- If things are going effortlessly, without force or manipulation, chances are it's right.
- As long as there's a green light or an open door, proceed ahead. Go through it. Chances are it's right.

Remember, you must learn to listen to your inner knowing-self as things are not always crystal clear. The magnificence that the universe has given you is freedom and power of choice: take that away and you are nothing but a mere robot. Bless your choices and choose with your inner knowing and wisdom.

TOOLS FOR COMMUNICATION

Some simple tools to begin the process of communicating with the higher conscious mind are:

- ⊙ Meditation
- ⊙ Singing
- ⊙ Rituals
- ⊙ Prayer
- ⊙ Dancing
- ⊙ Storytelling or Metaphors

These types of activities open the door to the sixth sense and activate a higher expansion and awareness.

Eighty percent of what we see in front of us and what we call our reality lies behind our eyes. We filter what we see through our memories of things that have already happened. We filter through our dogmas of how things ought to be, and we filter through our feelings about how things are. Thus, we look at what is going on through lenses ground by our hopes and by our fears.

There are many powerful techniques to go behind our eyes and communicate with our higher conscious mind.

> **I SHUT MY EYES IN ORDER TO SEE.** Paul Gamarin

Going into the Silence

Learning to go into the "silence" establishes a doorway of communication between your minds.

- ⊙ Go to a quiet place where you can sit or lie down for 15 minutes of silence. Do not talk, write or read, and try to think as little as possible; put your mind in neutral.
- ⊙ Imagine that your mind is like a body of water, and see how quiet and smooth you can make it so there is not a ripple.
- ⊙ When you have attained a quiet state, begin to listen for the deeper sounds of peace and harmony that are found in the heart of the silence.
- ⊙ Fill your mind with as many peaceful experiences and visualizations as possible. Then visit them deliberately.
- ⊙ The mind quickly responds, and it will give you a storehouse of productive thoughts, fresh ideas and a vast source of strength and power.

Practice this at least once a day to establish the connection between your minds and to start the communication process.

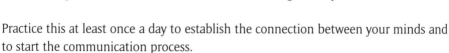

SILENCE IS THE ELEMENT IN WHICH GREAT THINGS FASHION THEMSELVES. THOMAS CARLYLE

BOOST YOUR CREATIVITY,
IMAGINATION AND INTUITION

The mind operates by the process of thinking. The mere creation of a thought causes the mind to react and then form an actual image. A vast range of imagery is available from the higher conscious mind. Imagery is one of the key jobs that the imagination carries out. To imagine something is the first step in the expression of the thought. It is where the magic begins. We are creative creatures, and our main job on earth is to create. When the combination of peace, relaxation and serenity is achieved, it puts you in touch with the higher self and the innate wisdom of your path and purpose.

The higher conscious mind knows why you are here. It is not judgmental, it only assists and guides you. It is the part of your mind that connects you with the "Larger Universal Mind" of which we are individuals and a subsystem. Some people call it the Spirit part of you. Understanding the value of being able to open the door to your higher mind and living your life by choice is sometimes difficult.

The late Sun Bear, a Native American teacher, once said: "The path of power is different for every individual … It is why you are here. When I speak of power, I mean a way of working and using all your energy – including your spiritual energy – in a direction that allows you to become a whole person, capable of fulfilling whatever vision the Creator gives to you. Finding your path of power is not always easy. For me to do it, I had to tear up both the white man's and the Indian's scripts for life. If you wish to walk the path of power, you must do the same."

As we communicate and access the higher levels of our consciousness, we go through levels that assist us in our pursuit of wisdom.

Brain research shows that stress and tension decrease the ability to access the intuition, imagination and creative part of your mind.

A PEACEFUL MIND GENERATES POWER. NORMAN VINCENT PEALE

THE SOUL–MIND CONNECTION

People are three-fold beings: body, mind, and soul.

- ⊙ The body is the manifestation of the soul, the miraculous mechanism, the physical appearance that you carry around and that can be seen.
- ⊙ The mind is our intellect, our memories, emotions, intuition, and our habits, beliefs and values.
- ⊙ The soul is what we refer to as the clothing of the spirit, which includes the mind.

The Soul–Mind is the super-conscious mind that is connected to your higher conscious mind. It is the mind that connects you to angels and spirit guides. The Soul–Mind holds and stores the memories of your genealogical heritage and, some believe, your past-life histories. It is the mind that has the spiritual understanding. Whether people openly admit it or not, they are on a spiritual search. At some time in their life, they will ask those questions, "Who am I?", "Why am I here?", "What is my purpose?", "What happens when I die?"

When we start questioning and seeking answers to these types of questions, we start reading more books and becoming more in tune, inquisitive and curious, and more responsible for our life and happiness. This opens up the channel or doorway to that Soul–Mind Connection, and leads us to learn more and to grasp the true meaning of the information we are getting as we apply it to ourselves. It enables us to become consciously aware of our divine spirit within.

> **CREATIVITY INVOLVES BREAKING OUT OF ESTABLISHED PATTERNS IN ORDER TO LOOK AT THINGS IN A DIFFERENT WAY.** Edward de Bono

INSPIRING PERSPECTIVES

Whether you are aware of it or not, you have the ability to observe life from more than one viewpoint or perspective. Being able to observe situations from different perspectives gives you a different viewpoint and a different experience. It also helps to increase creativity, improve emotional balance, and expand mental ability.

Imagine how enlightened you could be and how it would open your awareness and higher conscious mind.

The three perceptual positions

Position One
From a person's own experience, as if it were happening now.

Position Two
From another person's point of view or by stepping outside of the self for self-observation.

Position Three
An observer viewpoint watching the interaction between yourself and the other person.

Perspectives to Expand Creativity,
Imagination and Intuition

This exercise allows you to go beyond the normal perspective of a situation. You can take virtually any question or situation into this exercise and get "enlightenment" or guidance.

- ⊙ Think of something that you need clarity about.
- ⊙ Mark out three places in a line that represent the three different perceptual positions.
- ⊙ Standing in Position One: Looking at this from your own point of view, ask "How do I feel about this?", "What can I do to change this?" Record your answers.
- ⊙ Go to Position Two: Imagine becoming another person who can look at the same thing, but from his or her own point of view. Imagine as you become this other person, that you can turn and look at yourself in Position One. Notice how the other person perceives you and the situation; often you can sense how he or she feels and sees it.
- ⊙ Go to Position Three: Imagine you are a complete outsider, and you are looking at the people in Position One and Position Two. How does the person in Position Three see this situation, and what is his or her advice?
- ⊙ Go back to Position One: With all the information and knowledge gathered in each position, ask your higher conscious mind for advice and guidance now. Know that when it enlightens you, you will be aware.

Guidance Through Dreams, Visions and Meditation

Dreams and visions are both unconscious and higher conscious brain functions. They are usually not within our conscious control until we decide to train our minds to use them. By using our imaginations and opening our vision, we can learn to communicate with and direct our wise inner tutor.

Have you noticed that nothing seems to be impossible to the creators of the world? They seems to have far-reaching dreams with boundless vision. People such as Nelson Mandela, Thomas Edison, Abraham Lincoln, Henry Ford, and Martin Luther King did not just accept the way the "real" world was; they had dreams and beliefs in something better. Even in seemingly impossible situations, they dreamt on. The prerequisite for dynamic leaders, inventors and creative thinkers is that they all have the ability to imagine, visualize and dream.

A creative imagination triggers your higher conscious mind and opens up your visionary capabilities, which activate your dreams. Visualizations trigger the right brain's capacity to renew and change. It is a way of utilizing the vast array of imagery that empowers us.

Visualization techniques are extremely effective – they open our minds to a different dimension that evokes the inner tutor, wise counselor and advisor. They influence and activate the wondrous creative imagination. Just as affirmations put us in contact with the higher conscious mind, so do visualizations. Imagine your higher conscious mind quickening and releasing the information, then flooding the energy that is stored in your higher conscious mind to your whole brain. This is when you have enlightened experiences and intuition and hunches. Sometimes we get goose bumps or see a flash of light.

DREAM POWER

Everyone dreams, whether he or she realizes it or not. Dreams are natural representations of the unconscious and higher conscious minds.

There are two kinds of basic dreams.

- ⊙ The dream that makes no sense as the unconscious mind gets rid of unnecessary data accumulated during the day. These dreams usually have no significance and are harder to remember. This is where we release tension and stress.
- ⊙ The dream that, when you wake up, seems so real. It has a lot of symbolism. You just seem to know that it has a message. These types of dreams contain information, inspiration and guidance.

Begin to train your mind to remember your dreams. Keep a pen and paper by your bed so you can record them. Periodically review the dreams to see if there are any parallels to your life now, or messages for you. Interpreting your own dreams is a simple task once you start.

Take control and start to program yourself to have what is called lucid dreams. Simply say "I'm going to remember my dreams and be involved in them."

Lucid dreams are those where you have conscious awareness that you are dreaming, but you can control the content and sometimes sequence of your dreams. Some people levitate and fly in their lucid dreams. There is a Malaysian tribe called the Senoi, who are taught from childhood how to control individual factors in their lucid dreams to have beneficial outcomes. By consciously managing the lucid dreams, they get positive results in their real waking world, and handle their daily challenges with more ease.

COLOR AND CREATIVE VISUALIZATION MEDITATION

✳ Sit or lie in a quiet, comfortable position with your eyes closed. Think of the thing you wish to have help with. Then imagine it in a golden bubble outside your head.

✳ Begin to breathe deeply and relax; as you do, imagine a shaft of pure white light that is just above your head shining down upon you, engulfing your entire body with this radiant light.

✻ Breathe in this pure white light, letting yourself be filled with the light.

✻ Imagine a ball of pale purple just at the crown of your head, and breathe in this color, allowing it to open your connection to the higher universal wisdom.

✻ Move your attention to your third-eye area, or the center of your forehead, and visualize the color of dark purple or violet, breathing it in.

✻ Slowly move to the throat area, and imagine breathing in the warmth of dark blue, allowing it to resonate and emanate from your throat as you exhale.

✻ Gently move your attention to your heart area, and breathe in the rich color of green.

✻ Imagine a golden-yellow light glowing around the middle of you and, as you breathe in this radiant color deeply, let it flow through you.

✻ Next, bring your attention to your abdomen, and breathe in the vibrant color of orange. Imagine a deep orange color swirling and blending through you.

✻ Move your awareness to the base chakra, or pelvic area. Imagine the bright color of red and breathe in this color and allow it to flow through you.

✻ Finally, imagine breathing in the pure white light that surrounds you from the top of your head to the tips of your toes. Allow it to light you up inside and out. Now engulf the golden bubble with this light.

✻ As you focus on the golden bubble, notice how you feel and think about the thing with which you wanted help. Ask your higher conscious mind to assist you with clarity now. When you are ready, open your eyes.

COMMUNICATING WITH YOUR
HIGHER CONSCIOUS MIND

This process brings you into a state of awareness and a feeling of wholeness. It connects all three minds.

- ⊙ Find a place where you can relax. Close your eyes.
- ⊙ Imagine a shining ball of light hanging just above the top of your head. Imagine it is full of light, all the colors of the rainbow. It is spinning with light, color and pure energy from your super-conscious mind.
- ⊙ Ask the ball of light to send a beam of light down through the top of your head, down through your spine, down your legs and through your feet through the floor and to the center of the earth.
- ⊙ As you take in your next breath, take the energy from the center of the earth in through your feet to a place in the middle of your chest, and allow the energy to rotate there like a tiny ball of light.
- ⊙ Allow that energy to grow and fill all your cells; see it expand inside your body, filling every atom and molecule.
- ⊙ Allow your awareness to follow the light up your spine and up to the shining ball of light.
- ⊙ Now, imagine going to where the core of you resides. Go there now. Feel how good it is to connect to the innermost you.
- ⊙ Ask your higher conscious mind anything you wish, for guidance and assistance. Feel the peace, and listen to the silence inside of you.
- ⊙ When you are ready, come back to the real place, with your awareness in pace with your own rhythm and in your own time.

LIVING ON PURPOSE

Often we reach a stage in life when we feel like we are looking for meaning or "purpose." At these times we may be entrenched in our woes or feel embattled by circumstances and ask the question "why?" or "why me?" However, asking "why" questions only leads you to receive a lot of "why" reasons and excuses. It is by asking "how" questions rather than "why" questions that helps us to participate more fully in life. Ask: "How can I participate more fully in life?", "How can I become more fully conscious?"

We don't have to create passion or purpose. These are already within us. Often purpose is masked by fear, anxiety, or entrenched beliefs. We often break through these when we are fed up with the old ways, or when our old beliefs don't work for us anymore. This is the point when we begin to have purpose, and start particpating in life as a fully conscious being.

Living "on purpose" empowers you to use your brain to its full potential. Living "on purpose" means that you make your decisions; not other people or circumstances.

Seven Ways to Live on Purpose

1. BE WILLING TO TAKE CALCULATED RISKS.

Start with a strong hunch about something and intuitive knowing, and a willingness to do enough homework to make an informed decision. Someone once defined a hunch as a "conclusion based on facts stored on some unconscious belief." There is a difference between taking a calculated risk and being rash, between intuition and "into-wishing."

Build an enhanced intuition. Be aware of such information and curious about life. Feel certain feelings about a particular goal, and be willing to bring together all the available resources to turn what may have been a rash decision into a calculated risk with a high probability of success.

2. GO WITHIN TO YOUR INNER SILENCE FOR AT LEAST 15 MINUTES EACH DAY. BUILD THIS TO 30 MINUTES.

This will reduce your stress, and allow you to get in touch with the real you. Living from the inside out is essential.

3. LISTEN TO THE VOICE WITHIN.

This will be your voice. Your intuition is the voice of spirit, and it responds to your core beliefs to give you what you project.

4. REACH OUT TO OTHER PEOPLE; NETWORK.

Two or more heads are better than one. Two or more sets of hands can carry more water. It's not using people that works, it's reaching out, and giving and being in the flow.

5. OPTIMIZE OPPORTUNITIES. EXPLORE THE POSSIBILITIES.

Take a second look at things to see past the first impressions to the details and the larger picture and possibilities.

Ask the "what if" question. In China, there is no word for the concept of problem or challenge. When confronted with a situation, the Chinese use a word that means opportunity. A challenge and an opportunity can be the same thing, depending on how we view it. The same energy moves us forward from the challenge into the opportunity.

6. DO THE WORK AND TAKE ACTION

Keep on keeping on. Don't give up. Remember Thomas Edison and his ability to keep on keeping on in the face of seeming failure upon failure.

7. SUBMIT EVERY LIFE DECISION TO THE "VISION TEST."

Go within and just listen. "Just do it." Hold your vision clearly in mind, trust your higher conscious mind, and step up with confidence.

> THE CHALLENGE OF THE JOURNEY IS NOT THE DISTANCE WE GO,
> BUT THE PROCESS OF DISCOVERING WHO WE ARE WHEN WE GET THERE.
> THE IMPORTANT JOURNEY IS THE JOURNEY OF DISCOVERING SELF.

Glossary

ANTIOXIDANTS Active compounds that are found mainly in fresh fruits and vegetables and whole grains.

BRAIN HEMISPHERES The division of the brain into two main sections, each having its own function. Each operates semi-independently although they are physically connected.

CONSCIOUS MIND The place in the mind where a person is aware of his or her thoughts. It is in charge of the cerebrospinal nervous system.

CORPUS CALLOSUM A bundle of axonic fibers that connects two sides of the central nervous system.

HIGHER CONSCIOUS MIND Advice, guidance and data from this part of the mind is felt as intuition and gut feelings.

HIPPOCAMPAL COMMISSURE The axonic fiber that connects the link between the two halves of the brain hemispheres.

INTUITION Having the knowingness of something without conscious knowledge, such as a hunch.

ITERATE Movement back and forth between the brain structures. It takes place through the corpus callosum, which connects the two brain hemispheres.

LEFT BRAIN It is attached to the five senses. It is logical, analytical and rational. It uses rational language, and relates to science and mathematics.

MEDITATION Quiet contemplation and freeing the mind of inner chatter. Going within to the inner silence.

NEUROLOGY The study of the nervous system and its structure.

NEURON The basic conducting unit of the nervous system. Referred to as a nerve cell.

NEUROTRANSMITTER A chemical that transmits impulses from neuron to neuron.

NUTRIENTS Substances that nourish and promote growth.

PHYSIOLOGY The human body and how it moves and holds itself.

RIGHT BRAIN Perceives feelings and dominates emotions. Is creative and appreciates dance, art, music, and sculpture. Dominates the intuition and psychic senses. Controls the imagination faculty.

SPIRITUAL Having to do with the spirit or soul apart from the body.

SYNTAX A set of rules and steps for arranging or doing something.

UNCONSCIOUS MIND Referred to as the subconscious. The part of the mind that records and holds all memory in the conscious and higher conscious mind, that is experienced from all the senses.

This edition published by Barnes & Noble Inc.,
by arrangement with Lansdowne Publishing Pty Ltd

2002 Barnes & Noble Books
Reprinted 2002

ISBN 0-7607-3231-0

M 10 9 8 7 6 5 4 3 2

© Copyright 2002 Lansdowne Publishing Pty Ltd

Commissioned by Deborah Nixon
Production Manager: Jane Kirby
Text: Laureli Blyth
Illustrator: Penny Lovelock, additional illustrations by Sue Ninham, Joanna Davies,
Jane Cameron and Tina Wilson
Cover Illustration: Penny Lovelock
Designer: Avril Makula
Editor: Patricia Dacey
Project Coordinator: Bettina Hodgson

Set in Memento and Stone on QuarkXPress
Printed in Singapore by Tien Wah Press (Pte) Ltd